Advanced Praise for

B.O.S.S. RIGHTS

"*B.O.S.S. Rights* is a must-read for anyone who has doubted themselves because of childhood experiences and deep-rooted insecurities. You don't need to be perfect to make your mark in this world. You just need to be a willing vessel."

Theresa A. Burrage,
Author of About: *Things of Love, Life, Singleness and Other Stuff*

≈

"This book is exceptionally written and is an essential reading manual for anyone who's in a position of leadership or has the desire to lead or teach."

Kire Senoj,
Author of *My Mind's Eye vol.1: Life, Pain & Love.*

≈

"With the world going through so many trials related to its moral compass we need this. If you are looking for an encouraging word that inspires you to change the world-BOSS Rights is it."

Dr. Jeffery T. Burgin, Jr. Co-Owner,
2nd Timothy Consulting & Higher Education Professional

"I appreciated not only the lessons learned but also the tools provided throughout B.O.S.S. Rights. This book will serve as a guide to leaders who are searching for deeper connections personally and professionally."

Dr. Zaria Davis,
Senior Consultant & Spiritual Coach of New Direction Coaching & Consulting, LLC

≈

Childhood traumas (i.e., bullying, rape, incest, abuse,) tend to stifle the growth of adults who appear to have it all together. Without first recognizing we have issues and getting the necessary help to free ourselves from them, we will be forever trapped in our minds as wounded children.

B.O.S.S. Rights speaks to anyone with some of these experiences and serves as a guide to help individuals "BOSS-UP" to become the people God created us to be. This book spoke to my soul and helped me recognize where I have fallen short in my healing.

Shiwana Rucker
Author, Editor, and CEO of A Girl and Her Pen

B.O.S.S. RIGHTS

B.O.S.S. RIGHTS

A Leader's Guide to Recognizing that You are Built for Opportunities, Success and Service

B.O.S.S. Rights: A Leader's Guide to Recognizing that You are Built for Opportunities, Success, and Service

Copyright © 2023 by La'Shaunda Ewing

ISBN: 979-8-9875947-0-4

Published by: WisdomFlows, LLC.
Printed in the United States of America

Author Photos: Matthew (Salt) Postell and Victoria Evans

Internal Layout and Design: InSCRIBEd Inspiration, LLC.

Edited by: Theresa Burrage, Dr. Zaria Davis, Penda L. James, Erik Jones, Shiwana Rucker, Dr. Jeffrey Burgin

Cover Art: Le'Amaj Studioz. LLC

All real-life anecdotes are told with permission from the actual parties involved and recorded to the best of the author's recollection. Names, in some instances, have not been used at the request of the individuals referenced. In some cases, the parties mentioned are deceased. Details of some instances have been slightly modified to enhance readability or to ensure privacy. Any resemblance of any other parties is purely coincidental.

All rights reserved. No part of this book may be reproduced or transmitted in any form, electronic or mechanical, including photocopying and recording, or held in any information storage and retrieval system without permission in writing from the author and publisher.

Scripture is taken from the Amplified Bible, Copyright © 1954, 1958, 1962, 1964, 1965, 1987 by The Lockman Foundation, used by permission.

Scripture is also taken from King James Version, used by permission.

DEDICATION

I dedicate this book to Mercedes. She was a beautiful young lady with so much potential and a great light to those who knew her. Her life was taken by her own hand. That experience allowed me to see why I need to empower others to remember their worth and God-given purpose to impact the world around them.

B.O.S.S. RIGHTS

Contents

Overcoming Barriers To Success 1
   Who Is Lying To You? 3
   Winning While Losing 11
   The Purpose In Your Pain 15
   The Season Of Separation 23
   Know Your Rights 33

Make B.O.S.S. Moves 43
   The Characteristics Of A B.O.S.S. 45
   Built For This 49
   Open For Opportunities 59
   Success Is A Process 67
   Service Is A Priority 73

Conclusion 79

WHAT DO YOU BELIEVE?

*"Change will not come if we wait for some other person or some other time.
We are the ones we've been waiting for.
We are the change that we seek."*
~Barack Obama

Serving other people is one of the gifts that I rely on, and it brings me peace. When I serve others, it becomes a source of fuel, energy, and life for me. When I serve others, I can see them blossom and become successful, and I get to encourage them in their greatness. When opportunities surround me to lead, it is often with joy that I will step up to the forefront when others step back.

People often ask me to conduct trainings and workshops for my Sorority, ministry groups, church events, and community activities. Through public speaking, I began recognizing a call on my life to help other people realize their greatness. That is when I started teaching people about B.O.S.S. Rights. I define the term B.O.S.S. using an acronym: Built for Opportunities, Success, and Service.

Built for
Opportunities
Success &
Service
B.O.S.S.
RIGHTS

    In the past, I have struggled to recognize that there is God-given brilliance in me. Part of my problem was (and still can be) procrastination and perfection. I used to delay completing a project if I did not believe it was perfect or if people would approve. Recently, my therapist told me that I might have adult-onset ADHD. Because of that, sometimes, I become overwhelmed with tasks and inward thoughts of what is next. So I have to be intentional about creating checklists, positive self-talk, and having a coach or a mentor to hold me responsible for my success.

That is why I am writing this book; I want to remind you of the greatness within you. You are worthy, and it is time to take your skills and abilities to the next level. It is time for you to allow your gifts and talents to make room for you to become a leader and mentor in any space you occupy. We all have the opportunity right now to boss up.

Some of you have walked in self-doubt for way too long. You don't think you have enough credentials. You believe that you are less than and that somebody else is better than you. And actually, the reality is that you are even better than you believe. Black women are strong. Women run this world.

Say this statement out loud:

I AM A B.O.S.S.

A lot of us are winning while we are losing, yet there is purpose in our pain. So I hope you are ready for change.

ACKNOWLEDGEMENTS

First giving honor to **God,** who made this possible. You took my mess and made it a message, which took my test and gave me testimonies. You took my pain and gave it purpose. Thank you, Lord, for allowing me to see this day and for writing this book to inspire others to understand that they have been Built for Opportunities, Success, and Service. Thank you for allowing me to experience growth and letting my latter be greater.

Diana Ewing—To the woman who gave birth to me and is a whole BOSS. I've watched you overcome so much by not giving up but pushing through to make sure that your child had the opportunities afforded me while being my number one cheerleader. Thank you for all the sacrifices and prayers. Thank you for showering me with love. Mom, I love you, and I hope I made you proud.

Robert Hogan and Brenda Hogan—Thank you for being there my whole life! For genuinely being supportive, concerned, a sounding board for big decisions, and there for every big moment.

To the rest of my family by blood or adopted who has been by my side in one way or another— **My father, aunts, uncles, siblings, nieces, nephews, and cousins**. I love you. If you do not see your name charge it to my head and not my heart. Thank you for impact on my life!

Penda James—To my little sister who saw me and said, "God said to write the book." It was urgent and necessary. You keep saying I inspire you, but no, you let the Lord use you to make this come to pass. You felt like you weren't pushing me far enough at the time. But you exceeded the call of duty and got me right to the finish line. So I dedicate this book to you also. I love you to life, and you can do nothing about it.

Bridgette Rooks—Thank you for taking a phone conversation and completing my business blueprint. You were patient, honest and flexible. I thank GOD for you and Penda connecting us. I look forward to all of what we're going to do to make my business a success and blessing those who need to boss up.

Willie Franklin—You are one of the most gifted people on the planet, and sometimes you don't understand how creative and pure genius runs through your veins. Thank you!

To those who helped edit this book and provide encouragement along the way—I am forever grateful for your knowledge, time, prayers, and efforts **Dr. Zaria Davis, Dr. Jeffrey Burgin, Erik Jones, Theresa Burrage, and Shiwana L. Rucker.**

First Baptist Church of Kennedy Heights—to my covering for over 40 years, this is where I perfected my praise, my purpose, and the call on my life. Church family, I pray I've represented and served you well over the years.

The PSers —To my friends that I call family, a group of Bosses, people who are exceptional in every area of their lives but still know how to have a good turn-up.

Epsilon Lambda Sigma Chapter and Sigma Gamma Rho Sorority, Inc. —Thank you, Sisters, Sorors, Friends and Family for allowing me to try out so many of my techniques in this book over my 30 years of service to Cincinnati and this sisterhood with. Thank you for supporting me in my big moments and allowing me to shine bright. Too many names to call in this book, but I'll call you out publicly. And if you know, you know. Special Shout to the Soror who asked me at every conference, "Where is the book?"

To a few Bosses in Corporate America who truly allowed me to blossom—**Francine Yee, Bill Kaforey, Cassandra Moon, Kathy Burkett, Pamela Bingham, and Jodie Heflin**

To those who have gone on—To **both Mrs. Williams** at St. Joseph, **Willie and Marie Hill, Mattie Ewing, Arthur Ray Ewing, Eloise Hogan, and Margaret Leier, Todd Jones, Hakim Kent, Erica Embry, Rev. Edward Jackson, and Rev. Earl Wagner.** I genuinely wish you all could be here for this moment. I miss you more than you know.

OVERCOMING BARRIERS TO SUCCESS

WHO IS LYING TO YOU?

When dealing with my student Mercedes' sudden death, I was sitting at a table trying to comprehend how such a bright light would take her own life. Suddenly, continuous ticker tape statement scrolled across my eyes in midair as I sat at the table.

I could see it clearly:

Enough of the lies You Tell...
I am great.

What is after the ellipses in your life? Those three little dots can represent so many things. Do the dots represent your friends? Are your so-called friends jealous of how far you have progressed? Do they think that you have changed or that you are acting new?

Do the dots represent your family? Is someone telling you, "You act just like. . .?" You can fill in the blank. That comparison of you to someone else can cause you to live with the stigma of their dreams deferred or their mistakes that they try to associate with you. You can no longer live or accept those lies.

Is it the devil doing what the devil does? Which is to kill, steal, and destroy. The devil won't let you forget your past sins and failures, so you live a lie every day, trying to justify yourself and be the opposite of what the devil says about you.

Do the three dots represent you? Are you so busy trying to make everybody feel comfortable in your presence that you wear a mask? When did you last look in the mirror but didn't see yourself clearly? The Bible says, in I Corinthians 13:12, "or now we see through a glass, darkly." That means the object seen in the mirror can be skewed. Are you lying to yourself about your happiness, your success, your peace, or your insecurities?

For some of you reading this book today, you have more ellipses, those dot, dot, dots, than I can address in these short pages. People will talk, and if you're not careful, they will lead you astray because they are jealous. The reality is, when you look at yourself through God's eyes, greater is He that is in you than is He that is in this entire world. You no longer have to bow down to the lies spoken about you.

You don't have to be tripped up and stuck because of someone or something that is trying to hinder you. Set yourself up for the greatness in your future by choosing to stand up for the truth of your purpose and your destiny.

The greatness that resides within you is always there. So often, people want to find favor with the world, allowing others who are jealous of their existence and anointing to speak death over them, look down upon them, and/or despise the blessings they have received. Stop complaining and recognize the blessings God has bestowed upon you.

RIGHTS
Exercise - Create a Checklist

. . . let us lay aside every weight, and the sin which doth so easily beset us, and let us run with patience the race that is set before us
Hebrews 12:1 (KJV)

Make a list of lies or generational curses that have been holding you back?

- _____
- _____
- _____
- _____
- _____
- _____
- _____
- _____
- _____
- _____

Now make a list of action steps to debunk them.

- _____
- _____
- _____
- _____
- _____
- _____
- _____
- _____
- _____

Read your list aloud and give it to God. Once you do this, these generational curses are no longer yours to carry.

Casting all your cares [all your anxieties, all your worries, and all your concerns, once and for all] on Him, for He cares about you [with deepest affection, and watches over you very carefully].

I Peter 5:7 (AMP)

Let's move forward . . .

Enough of the Lies You Tell

Throughout my personal and professional life, I have served people and helped them create success. But, when opportunities came toward me to achieve success, I overlooked them because of what other people were saying about me. I wanted people to see what I thought I could be to them. The problem was, I did not recognize that I didn't need to be anything to anybody other than myself.

I don't understand the fear of rejection that I struggled so hard to overcome. The B.O.S.S. was already inside of me, and because of that, I was built for opportunities, success, and service. I did not need their approval. I do not need anything, but the anointing, talent, and gifts God gave me to manifest themselves.

No one could make me be me because I was already created in God's image. He created me to be a B.O.S.S. and I wasted too much time and energy giving myself to others for their validation. I did not recognize at the time that my anointing and covering in God did not require anyone else's approval. I did not need my father or family to justify me to go forward with my life. I needed to show up and trust the process. I am good enough. I am worthy. I am a whole B.O.S.S. by design, predestined to lead.

Delayed, Not Denied

I thank God that delayed does not mean denied. The B.O.S.S. in me is standing tall. I look at myself here in 2022, writing this book ten years after beginning the journey. That is an example of God's gifts being given without repentance (Romans 11:29).

So many opportunities were overlooked, disregarded, not accepted because I was afraid, or I didn't think I was worthy. Today I recognize, I am walking confidently, and I am determined not to miss any more opportunities that God gives me.

So enough of those lies. I am great! I'm moving forward with the understanding that through the learning process from this missed opportunity, my purpose will be revealed and fulfilled.

It is important that I am surrounded by people who understand my plan and that the greatness within me has to be delivered to the world. My village prays for, and with me, they hold me accountable and remind me that God entrusted me with purpose and multiple gifts that make me great.

I am going to help you be the B.O.S.S. that is already within you with the confidence, the tools, and the strength to recognize that your first step has already been taken. You just have to walk it out.

Overcome The Barriers to Success:

- Recognize that lies will be told about you. It is your choice to believe them or not.
- Rely on and trust the vision that God has given you. Do not listen to the voices of other people

WINNING WHILE LOSING

Have you considered my servant . . .
Job 1:8

A friend of mine was once acknowledged as a finalist for the *Woman of the Year in Technology*. While sitting with her at the gala, surrounded by her family, who were together for the first time in a while, her friends, and coworkers, I noticed that my friend was acting unusual. This usually overly confident woman was on the verge of throwing up.

"What is going on?" I asked her.

She replied, "I'm just so nervous."

"What are you nervous about?" I replied.

"What if I don't win?"

"What do you mean?" I asked.

"What if I don't win? What if I don't get the award." I was trying to understand the problem because, in my mind, she had already won.

"There were probably 50 people who were nominated for this award. You are one of three finalists. Is that not a win?"

I looked around the room and said, "You have a whole table full of support right here. The fact that you were nominated lets us know that you are being set up for the come-up. Your name is being spoken throughout this room. Folks will leave here knowing your name and carry it. Whether you win the award or not, you have had wins along the way."

My friend smiled and said, "I will do my best to enjoy the rest of the night.

When the awards were announced, the bios of each nominee were read, starting from the third runner-up. My friend sighed after the second runner-up and said, "Oh God, I didn't win." As we watched the presentation, the top honoree's name appeared on the screen, and it was my friend! When they brought the award out, my friend's name was already engraved on it. She had been set up for the win but had no idea.

The world makes us think that we are losing, and all the time, the small wins are a setup for a big win. The lesson I learned that day is that when it looks like we are losing, God wants us to know He can turn anything around, so we win it all.

When my friend fretted about the possibility of not winning the award, she did not consider her small wins. She could not enjoy herself during the awards ceremony because she focused on the wrong thing. I'm telling you, as I told her, there is a process to defining your worth. Diamonds are made under pressure. Gold has no value until it is purified and cleaned. If you are in the fire right now, your worth is being refined.

"But he knows where I am going. And when he tests me, I will come out as pure as gold."

Job 23:10 NLT

Overcome The Barriers to Success:

- Stop looking at the people and your surroundings. You are predestined for greatness. Look to GOD and put your faith into action.
- Your small wins are a setup for a big win.

THE PURPOSE IN YOUR PAIN

The thief cometh not, but for to steal, and to kill, and to destroy: I have come that they might have life, and that they might have it more abundantly.
John 10:10

The story of Job in the bible is the blueprint of what it looks like to be set up to win. One thing you need to know is that there is always someone looking at your life and recognizing how blessed you are. They speak your name in places you have not stepped foot in because they see your courage and faith. So don't be surprised when everything seems to be going right and a test comes your way. In other words, the devil will show up because his job is to steal, kill and destroy (John 10:10).

Job wholeheartedly followed God; the scripture calls him blameless. He had God's divine protection, a great family, a thriving business, a large estate, good health, and a solid reputation. Job was prosperous. He had 7,000 sheep, 3,000 camels, 500 oxen, 500 donkeys, seven sons, and three daughters.

Things don't always happen because of the devil. Sometimes God wants to elevate you in the kingdom for His work.

One day Satan was walking amongst the sons of God talking, and he started talking about Job. God presented him to Satan because of his faith. In one night, Job lost it all: his house, cattle, livelihood, children, and health. Job 1:12 talks about the setup for Job's come up. After he lost it all, he was set up for a come-up. He stood up, tore his robe in grief, shaved his head, fell to the ground, and worshipped God. In all of this, Job did not sin by blaming God.

Job tried to convince his friends that he had done nothing wrong to deserve what was happening to him. They did not understand, but he knew his pain had a purpose; Job's faith never wavered.

Everything that you have gone through is part of your purpose. Stop throwing pity parties because things are going wrong. Thank God for your blessings, even things you lost along the way. You can't add more to an already full cup.

Level Up

While Job trusted God, his wife tried to tell him to curse God and die. She could not handle his anointing. Thankfully, Job responded to his wife with the assurance of his faith. "I know that my redeemer lives" (Job 19:25).

Are you listening to God or people for the answers? Do you have friends or family members who only know how to tell you exactly what you don't want to do? Make sure you're in a relationship with the One who knows and sees all.

Look at your situation through God's eyes. God's thoughts are not our thoughts. His ways are not our ways, and you must have the same confidence in God that Job had. Not everyone understands the call, so be careful whom you share your vision with to protect your focus and faith. This will allow the B.O.S.S. to rise up without distractions, and it will keep you strong.

Are you prepared to level up for yourself and for your family to win? Like Job, you may be chosen to change things in your family and within your bloodline. You may be chosen to carry the weight of the anointing and favor, which is a gift from God.

Consider what it says in Ecclesiastes 3: 1-4:

To everything there is a season,
and a time to every purpose under the heaven:
A time to be born and a time to die; a time to plant, and a time to pluck up that which is planted.

A time to kill, and a time to heal; a time to break down, and a time to build up.
A time to weep, and a time to laugh.
A time to mourn, and a time to dance.

When you are in a troublesome situation, be intentional about responding to your circumstance with faith first. If you find yourself jumping to the wrong conclusions or only seeking the wrong advice, learn to trust God.

What happens to you is for your good, even when it doesn't always feel like it.

> *"Let us not become weary in doing good,*
> *for at the proper time, we will reap a harvest if we do not give up."*
> Galatians 6:9

Pain in life is inevitable; Job can tell you that. But in the end, he got double for his trouble. He was winning when he thought he was losing. One of my favorite scriptures is I Peter 5:10. I like the Amplified Version:

After you have suffered for a little while, the God of all grace [who imparts His blessing and favor], who called you to His own eternal glory in Christ, will Himself complete, confirm, strengthen, and establish you [making you what you ought to be].

This scripture tells me that pain, struggles, and hardships will not last always. When you endure and don't abort the lessons, your promises received will be worth the trouble. Be like Job, trust in God, and spend time with Him. Your anointing is not dependent upon anyone else's approval.

    God trusts you and recognizes that you trust Him. God favors you, and He knows that you will cry, but you will praise Him through the storm. God has no doubts about you, but you may have to sit in the middle of a mess that will become a profitable message. But, like Job, there will be times when you must convince people that God's grace and wisdom are still abundant, even during a tragedy.

    Do not fight God for taking away what no longer belongs to or benefits you. Do not give up or sit on the sidelines and watch life happen. Instead, press into your purpose and align yourself with people who know how to pray and create avenues for you. The purpose in your pain is the foundation of who you are as a B.O.S.S.

    If you are thinking you have lost, you have already won.

Overcome The Barriers to Success:

- Don't abort the process; it is for your perfection. If God brought you to it, you will get through it.
- Always make sure you are intentional about how you respond – faith first.

THE SEASON OF SEPARATION

    I recently had a conversation with my brother about how sometimes God must take a person away from their friends and family for quality time so that He can speak to them. We talked about how sometimes in life, we have to be set apart in order to be saved. In my brother's case, for a season, he was separated from friends and family who were telling him who he was supposed to be. And while he was incarcerated, he was able to listen to God and allow Him to remind Him who he is.
    Just like my brother needed a time of separation to save his life and hear from God, you too may need a time of separation. Use that time, without distractions, to get direction for your purpose and keys to success. Decide to either live the life that God gave you or choose to let fear and negativity distract you from seeing the promises of God fulfilled in your life.

"The Spirit immediately drove him out into the wilderness,"

Mark 1:12

Thinking about my brother, I started to reflect on Jesus being in the wilderness for 40 days. Author Don Schwager called it "a place of testing, encounter, and renewal." Jesus was without food in the wilderness to prepare himself for the mission the Father had sent him to accomplish. Separation is different from being alone. Being isolated from the distractions of this world (e.g., cellphones, social media, naysayers) allows you the opportunity to hear and prepare for your purpose. Do not neglect stillness so you can hear from the universe.

When we are weak, we are strong in God. Nothing is going on in your life that God doesn't know about, nor is there anything God's power cannot take away. We must acknowledge where we are so we can receive His help. That means we need to stop denying our weaknesses.

Plus, if we talk about them openly, other people can't hold us hostage to them.

When you make it out of a trying situation, tell your testimony. When you testify, you become a mirror for someone else. When God brings you out, avoid some people, and the places you came from that were stumbling blocks. Remember, separation can be a necessary blessing. Don't look back, or you might turn into salt like Lot's wife.

We tend to judge people on a surface level, the book by the cover, which means we have no understanding of the person's inside, their true nature, because of outside appearances or influences.

The Test of Separation

When we started school, we were given levels to achieve before advancing to the next grade. Along the way, some people struggle in school because they don't communicate with their teachers to properly prepare for the tests. In Isaiah 30:20-21, we are given instructions for how to handle tests.

Stop looking at your problems and look to your Teacher. This is the only way that you will understand that your problems are temporary. If the Lord is the teacher, trust Him with your pain:

And though the Lord give you the bread of adversity, and the water of affliction, yet shall not thy teachers be removed into a corner anymore, but thine eyes shall see thy teachers: And thine ears shall hear a word behind thee, saying, This is the way, walk ye in it, when ye turn to the right hand, and when ye turn to the left.

(Isaiah 30:20-21(ASV).

Teachers have responsibilities to their students:

1. **Mentor** - An effective teacher understands that their part is to be consistent, engaged, genuine, and aligned with the student's needs.
2. **Educate**- Teachers give students intellectual, moral, and social instruction on better ways of achieving using various tools to reach their goals.
3. **Motivate** - Teachers spend countless hours making students feel determined, loved, ready to accomplish goals, and enthusiastic about victories.
4. **Guide** - Teachers provide information and insights that help students make the most of the experience and move in the direction with the most benefits.
5. **Lead** - Teachers show the way. They provide vision and the path to realizing it. Teachers ensure their students have support and create opportunities to see greatness within themselves.

In your current position, are you asking for help? Are you listening? Are you preparing yourself for growth? Are you spending time with your Teacher?

Think about one teacher who helped you by opening themself up to a relationship with you. That teacher helped you understand the lesson and helped you recognize that you were ready for elevation. This principle is demonstrated in II Corinthians 4:16:

> *Therefore, we do not lose heart. Even though our outward man is perishing, yet the inward man is being renewed day by day. For our light affliction, which is but for a moment, is working for us a far more exceeding and eternal weight of glory, while we do not look at the things which are seen, but at the things which are not seen. For the things which are seen are temporary, but the things which are not seen are eternal.*

Reflecting During Separation

Every first Sunday, people go to church to take communion to commemorate what God has done for them. But, honestly, when was the last time you reflected on what God has done for you? I mean, really taken the inventory of the victories and the ways made?

If you get tripped up when you are going through something because you think God needs to do something different, look back, and you will see that He has brought you out before, but you must believe He will do it again. When you are going through something, say out loud, "This ain't new to you, God."

Perhaps you don't feel worthy of love, and that is why you feel defeated. Once you understand your worth, you will realize that you are worth everything Jesus died for. Romans 8:31 says, *"If God is for you, who can be against you?"*

Jesus suffered on the cross, yet He still got up. It is God who justifies us. You are more than a conqueror; what you are going through is because God wants you to be everything He has called you to be —there is pain in your purpose.

My Test of Faith

While writing this book, my faith was tested. A whirlwind of events happened in my life within a 30-day period. First, I was hospitalized for Atrial-Fabulation (when the heart beats too fast). Second, I had severe back pain, which caused me to struggle to walk, sit, and sleep. The impact of this pain also caused issues with controlling my bodily functions. I had X-Rays, and an MRI to find the source of the problem. They gave me injections to help with the pain. From the results of the scans, I discovered I have a herniated disc in my back.

Around the same time, I was also diagnosed with a small growth on my throat called a polyp, and I had to see a specialist. My voice is a big part of my ministry. I teach, sing, and preach, so I had to stand on my faith. I prayed, "Listen here, Jesus, if you called me to this, you must get me through this." I recognized that this was my time to be still and separate. So I said, "What is my part to play in all of this?"

As Job's story closes in chapter 42, he confesses to God what he believes about himself. Job realizes he wasn't as intimate with God as he should have been. That led to doubt and fear. So in your season of separation, allow God to strengthen you.

Overcome The Barriers to Success:

- If Jesus needed a time of testing and separation for His perfection, so you do you.
- Distractions are things that separate you from your purpose. If you can't live without them, limit them, or completely remove them.

"You can't make big moves if you're easily stumped by small thinking."

~Rene Rodrigez

B.O.S.S. RIGHTS

KNOW YOUR RIGHTS

For I know the plans I have for you," declares the Lord, "plans to prosper you and not to harm you, plans to give you hope and a future.
Jeremiah 29:11

One time when I was driving, a crazy light flickered in my Chevy Trailblazer. I called the Chevy dealer and explained, "I don't know what's going on. This is really peculiar."

When the mechanic asked, Have you read the owner's manual?" I had to admit that I hadn't done that to figure out the problem. The information I needed to know about that light was right at my fingertips. When I read the manual, I realized it was a simple fix, and I could do it myself without taking my car to the dealership for repairs.

That reminds me that we often have information available to us, but we don't use it. I see this all the time as a preacher. If I am preaching and my audience has not read the Bible, I can almost tell them anything true or untrue if I say it in a tone that moves them.

I tell people they need to study the bible for themselves to learn the God-given privileges that God has given them as His child. In II Timothy 2:15, the Bible says, *"study to show yourself approved."* Are you studying to understand your rights?

From God, you are given the responsibility to help others, to offer your ideas and speak your voice, to carry out God's mission, and to engage with others in a brotherly or sisterly way. I know, sometimes that can be scary to do. You can stretch yourself and walk while afraid by learning a new skill or offering your talents to create a win.

Know Your Rights In Groups

As a B.O.S.S., it is critical to study and be prepared for the next level of success. If you are a member of any group or organization, it is important to study the bylaws and read the organization's constitution. From the day you joined the group, you were given all rights and privileges for membership. When you study this information, it equips you to be a good member. Apply your knowledge, and people cannot threaten or intimidate you with false information. You can conquer doubt with knowledge. You can walk while you are afraid.

Robert's Rules of Order is used as a foundation to conduct business meetings. In Chapter 14, "The Role of a Member," the author describes what members should do by writing, "Unless members take an active role in the organization, it can't function or even exist." For example, if you are part of a group with members who do all the work, what happens when they get tired? The burden is on their shoulders.

If nobody runs for office or participates, your organization can go from growth, prosperity, and a good name in the community to dying out. Burnout can occur in members when everybody is not carrying their assigned or God-given role. Take heed from Ephesians 4:16 (ESV):

From whom the whole body, joined and held together by every joint with which it is equipped, when each part is working properly, makes the body grow so that it builds itself up in love.

Know Your Rights at Work

You go to a job, and you may work with people you don't like. Despite the hindrance of people, you are not deterred from your mission to make money. Your mind is set on accomplishing your goal, and your coworkers don't stop you. When you get up and get ready for work, you ask the Lord to give you peace, grace, and patience for the day. If you can do this on your job, you can do it in other areas of your life.

What do you do when you feel afraid? Do you move, or do you stay stagnant? Know that it is okay to walk while you are afraid. Think about some things that may cause you to feel stuck. When you seek clarity and direction, you figure out how to plan better, which breaks your stagnation.

RIGHTS
Exercise - Seek Clarity

What is keeping you from bringing your best self forward? Do you need clarity about something?
☐ Yes ☐ No

Are you burnt out, frustrated, or unheard?
☐ Yes ☐ No

Are you afraid or holding yourself back?
☐ Yes ☐ No

Are you overwhelmed with obligations?
☐ Yes ☐ No

Do you fear others won't accept your change?
☐ Yes ☐ No

Do you worry about resources or support?
☐ Yes ☐ No

Pick one area in your professional, personal, or organizational life where you can walk while afraid.

The Fail Fast Principle

Dale Carnegie once said, "Develop success from failures. Discouragement and failure are two of the surest stepping stones to success." I have seen this theory at work in my experience in Information Technology. We call it "Fail Fast." When something is not working, we believe it is okay to get the buoy and life raft for the team instead of going down on a sinking ship. Someone on the team will be courageous and say, "This is not working. I think we should try another way."

In this situation, don't try to drag other people down to prove a point. If you do that, you will waste time and money. It would be even worse if you knew what happened and acted ignorant by questioning others about what they did or did not do. With the Fail Fast principle, you recognize that it's okay to walk while afraid and even fail, but Harsh Bardhan Pandey wrote an article on his LinkedIn page to remind us, "never fail twice the same way[1]."

He states, "Failing is nothing to be ashamed of or to be annoyed. Failing the same way twice is. To approach the problem in various ways relentlessly is the true mark of a leader."

I have had many experiences where I needed to be honest with myself when I did not know what I was doing. In those moments, I decided to push myself because I did not want to let anyone on my team down in the pursuit of a goal. Failures provide us with lessons for the next opportunity to get it right.

Charles Osgood wrote a Poem called "Responsibility":

> *"There was an important job to be done, and Everybody was sure that Somebody would do it. Anybody could have done it, but Nobody did it. Somebody got angry about that because it was Everybody's job. Everybody thought Anybody could do it, but Nobody realized that Everybody*

---

[1] https://www.linkedin.com/pulse/never-fail-twice-same-way-differently-harsh-pandey/

wouldn't do it. It ended up that Everybody blamed Somebody when Nobody did what Anybody could have."

Who are you; Everybody, Somebody, Anybody, or Nobody? Regardless of who you think you are, you do not have to keep that name. Don't sit on the sidelines feeling like your talents are untapped while you criticize all the people stepping up to work. You see the B.O.S.S. in them, but you must activate it within yourself.

Get up and get to work.

Overcome The Barriers to Success:

- Walk like you are a B.O.S.S.
- Study to show yourself approved.
- Walk while you are afraid.

MAKE B.O.S.S. MOVES

THE CHARACTERISTICS OF A B.O.S.S.

I will praise thee; for I am fearfully and wonderfully made: marvelous are thy works; and that my soul knoweth right well.

Psalm 139:14

If you lead, you lead by example, even when you must make tough decisions. In leadership, you cannot be power-hungry. A good leader never leverages their power over others.

The Oxford Dictionary defines a boss as one who oversees a worker, group, or organization. Leaders must work with and for their constituents. Leaders can never ask anyone to go where they are unwilling to step first.

In Corporate America, we can all agree that a boss usually displays or carries the following characteristics:

- Depth of Knowledge
- Motivation
- Devotion

- Role Model
- Kind
- Understanding of strategy
- Respected
- Defines and understands vision and goals
- Supports the development and is invested in the growth of their team
- Values success of individuals
- Influence
- Develops a succession plan
- Courage
- Self-Awareness
- Gratitude

According to the Urban Dictionary, "Boss-Up" means "directing the full capacity of their time, resources, and attention toward a specific direction, goal, or intent. In other words: step up, raise your standard, up your game, and take responsibility for the direction of your life and the full maturity of your dreams."

What are you willing to do differently to become a B.O.S.S.?

Think Like a B.O.S.S.

If you work in Human Resources or own a business, when you recruit new people, you look for specific characteristics that will allow your business to flourish. For example, you hire employees to add value, contribute, and set yourself up for advancement. When you know your rights, you know the rules, expectations, and the direction the team is supposed to go.

Think about it like this if you are a spades player. The game's real advantage is having the Ace, King, Queen, Jack, or a 10 of spades. So you see these cards in your hand, you know that you are automatically set up for a win because they are in your hand.

The deck is what it is like when you know your rights. If something is out of order, you can use the right card (person or resource) to correct or shift the atmosphere and move in a different direction. For example, if you are playing and somebody thinks they have the advantage, but you have the King (your anointing or experiences), you can slap it down and bring light to the truth. What is in your hand, heart, and head can shift the circumstance and cause your team to win. You have no choice but to win if the deck is in your favor.

Stop comparing yourself to others. Let go of the imposter syndrome. You were created uniquely for this moment in time to create. What works best for you means that you must give your voice to what works best for you. People often want to change but base their change on other people and what they do. Change is inevitable, it is necessary, and it is good, but it must be intentional. Think about your personal brand and what you want five years from now. If that is too far out, dream big for this season and make the necessary shifts to accomplish them. Stop being your roadblock. You were built for this in God's image.

Overcome The Barriers to Success

- Do what it takes to be a B.O.S.S.
- When you lead, you must lead by example.

BUILT FOR THIS

Brethren, I count not myself to have apprehended: but this one thing I do, forgetting those things which are behind, and reaching forth unto those things which are before, I press toward the mark for the prize of the high calling of God in Christ Jesus.

Philippians 3:13-14 (KJV)

Growing up I thought I was cute, but thicker than most. My Grandfather's nickname for me was "Tub" because I was so big for my age.

As a child and teen, I was constantly made aware of my body. My family, friends, and of course, the kids at school pointed out when I was overeating (in their opinion), instructing me on how much I should weigh and reminding me when my clothes size kept going up. I remember going to grade school and seeing these thin girls with long hair and pretty skin. They were the in-crowd. I even went to high school with some of them. I always wanted to fit in but was constantly judged for my body. Thin was in. The pretty thin ones got the opportunities, while the thick ones were looked at as body parts.

I remember thinking to myself, "What do I gotta do to fit in? What do I gotta do to make people like me?" because clearly, I'm not set up for greatness because of the skin that I'm in. I was getting attention for all the wrong reasons. Not my intelligence and leadership skills but my looks that created insecurity in me. Not the God-given talents, even at a young age, that were trying to Boss Up.

I ran to the right crowd and the wrong crowd all at the same time. I was too smart for my own good to even fail. I'm grateful that my mother saw something in me that I couldn't always see in myself. I had secrets that would keep me from being set up for the come-up, or at least I thought. I was molested as a child. I kept that secret from my family; most will learn it when they read this book.

You walk around with these secrets and see and understand that those secret sins trap you from understanding your greatness and worth. I carried secrets into high school, not valuing who I was. And to be honest, some of my adulthood. I grew up in a single-parent household, not always feeling wanted by parts of my family. I was almost denied the greatness that would be revealed in me. I was not set up for the come-up because of the lies told about me or placed upon me.

I got through high school and went on to college, and I still tried to fit in. I'm older and stronger now, but still. I help others succeed but struggle to see my worth and value. Here is the catch, I was still leading while afraid and doubting. See, when GOD has his hand on you, you can't help but win because His purpose will be fulfilled. In college, I was President of my Sorority chapter, a choir director, and more because people saw in me at the time what I could not see in myself. My gift of service and helps lent itself to leadership because I want everyone to win. I put on a good face because I wore those masks and told myself lies. I didn't always succeed to the greatest heights possible, not because they were unavailable but because I was still just trying to see myself as special.

I've always looked at others to be like them and have what they had. Here comes the imposter syndrome again. As a full-figured black woman, I have experienced this world with people who have tried to tell me what I can achieve, how I should look, and even the men I can have. Because of this, I was a B.O.S.S. to everybody else but myself. But God!

The little girl in me did not recognize that she had always been a B.O.S.S. I was active in school and had a lot of opportunities. I always looked cute in my school pictures, but I struggled to understand why people didn't accept me, as I was overflowing with love and abilities. I guess I was a little bit too thick for their liking or understanding. But God.

Sometimes we are our own worst critics, and so in this world, I've tried to be everything to everybody else. I am a people pleaser; I know that for a fact. The devil played the insecurity game in my head—trying to be accepted by my family and friends. But the biggest hurt is not being accepted by your family. Love comes and shows up in so many facets that it is not always understandable. This can cause struggles in every area of your life and doubt your place, peace, and purpose. We just need to learn that blood does not always mean love. We have to press on with those who cherish and genuinely love us and see the abundance inside. And have several But God moments.

    I'm overcoming, and I must continue to walk it out. I see in my life that there are opportunities right before me. However, the People pleaser can make you think you are a Savior, thinking you can prove your value. Trying to prevent a friend from committing suicide, I was raped. Trying to be present for someone who was in danger caused me harm. That led me to a moment of questioning and trying to understand my worth. I realized again that being a good girl clearly would not keep me from trouble or make me fit in.

I kept telling myself the lie that people needed me, and I did not use discernment to avoid harmful situations that kept presenting themselves. Am I leaning to my own understanding and missing the B.O.S.S. within me?

Wow, but God, again.

Because of God's patience and some good therapy, I've received peace, wealth, and strength. The opportunity to help others has always been a blessing. People see me as a mother even though I've never birthed a child because I care enough to help them, see them, and then I understood that it wasn't even the lies that I was telling myself, but I had to help others see that there are lies they've been speaking into existence.

Rape is tragic. If you survived, it means you have a purpose, even while healing. You can handle challenges and help others overcome theirs, even while working through the process. We will see it through if we trust God, is taking us to our next B.O.S.S. level. That's a lie the enemy tries to tell you—that we are less than we are, because of the act, that we are not worthy, that we can't make it, that we can't achieve, and that we can't be better than the last generation. Own it and let the mess become your message.

Enough of those lies. We are great women; we are great men. We come from a people of Kings and Queens, stolen from their land, placed in slavery, and endured the Civil rights movement, who had to overcome so that we could Boss Up. We now must walk it out and be the bosses built for opportunities, success, and service for a time such as this. Your tests are now your testimonies. Your mess is now your message. Your valley will become your mountain. Your vice will become your victory!

Enough of the lies that have been told to us by the devil, our family, our so-called friends, and even ourselves. You are built for this. You are developed by the definition of the word built - "a systematic plan by a definite process, or on a particular base." Now, set your sights on something bigger and make B.O.S.S. moves.

You've got your rights. You understand your privileges and know the importance of creating an atmosphere for your healing and generational legacy. Now, you need to release your burdens so you can move forward and build your platform for service and success. Put your energy into what you want to do most, and you will shine bright.

If you feel burnt out, what do the people in your circle need to know to support you right now? You may have secret battles, and your confidence is low, but trust your circle. Be intentional about creating moments to connect with your village of supporters. God, and they have your back.

Learn how to create an atmosphere where you can be yourself. A true B.O.S.S. is not afraid to be around people who will tell them the truth when they are performing at a level less than excellent. If you want to change, being a B.O.S.S. means that sometimes you dare to have hard conversations with people when they, or you, are being steered away from greatness.

You may feel detached because you are going through something, but you must recognize that not every atmosphere is conducive to being transparent or your best self. Sometimes you have to take care of business that people are not equipped to help you.

Don't give up on yourself. You must recognize and take ownership of your faults, while others may see you as perfect. As long as you are genuine and humble, people will embrace you. As you lead, utilize your authority to make things easier for others and secure a foundation for them to stand on. Your leadership empowers the entire team to walk into new roles while afraid or because you have prepared them. Show your support for them publicly.

Overcome the Barriers to Success

- Seize the opportunities that are presented to you.
- Set your sights on something bigger and make B.OS.S. moves.

OPEN FOR OPPORTUNITIES

"You can keep either making excuses or start making moves."
~G Swiss

On one occasion, I ran into friends at the grocery store. We started discussing our visions, and I told them about an idea for an after-school program I wanted to implement. One of the friends shared that they had a program but were moving away. "Do you want to take over my after-school program?"

This person saw my worth and was excited to extend this opportunity to me. I took the news and started to share it with others. The questions were fired at me, "What kind of money are you going to make doing that?" Someone asked, "How much time is that gonna take? Are you gonna be able to keep up the lifestyle you are accustomed to on an after-school program salary?" There were so many questions I started to question myself, "Could I? Can I? Is this for me?"

Before talking to people who did not share my vision, I never had those questions in my mind. Once they were planted, even though God gave me the vision, I started to doubt. Because I was not rooted in my vision, I allowed people to make me question what God told me to do.

Then, I ended up turning it down because I did not trust the B.O.S.S. in me. I turned it down partially because I was in a career that, by worldly standards, was amazing. So how could I give it away for something that was not guaranteed?

This opportunity would have been a business I dreamed of because it would have fulfilled my passion. Doubt and other people's opinions caused me to lose. It was not because I was unworthy or not gifted but because I didn't trust myself or GOD's abilities in me.

I spoke with my friend recently at the prompting of the Spirit. I asked my friend a question that plagued me all these years, "Did I give away what was given to me freely?"

My friend said, "Yes, it was yours to take." He told me he was disappointed because he and his team knew I would be awesome. "We believed that God sent you," he said, "But we could not wait for you to walk it out." My friend clarified several things about my next stage of life: to be still and listen for God's "Yes!" and no one else.

"Then," he said, "God's direction will put you right on purpose and give you victory.

It was time for me to B.O.S.S. up!

This experience reminds me of what social media influencer Malcolm "MJ" Harris meant when he said, "Stop waiting for others to create those steps for you. You are the only person with the power to create the life you desire for yourself." I agree with this sentiment wholeheartedly.

Merriam-Webster defines an opportunity as "a favorable juncture of circumstances; a good chance for advancement or progress."

Are you holding on to baggage that is weighing you down and preventing you from seeing the opportunities in front of you? Some things are not meant to go into your future. Let them go before they bleed into other areas of your life. Has someone caused you heartache, and do you feel the need to get back at them? If so, you are harming yourself more than you are harming them.

You are blessed with skills and talents. Take inventory of your skills and execute your goals. Do what you can to be Godly and live on purpose because you are royalty.

Your job as a leader is to motivate your team on a shared vision while making the journey enjoyable, educational, and purposeful. Leaders recognize that not everyone will willingly follow them. In those situations, they can show the opportunities in front of them to be great and leverage others to encourage them. True leaders are not afraid to share the spotlights with others and delegate for growth for all. True leaders look for opportunities to lead.

Overcoming The Barriers to Success

- Stop comparing yourself to others and start competing.
- Look for opportunities to lead.

B.O.S.S. RIGHTS

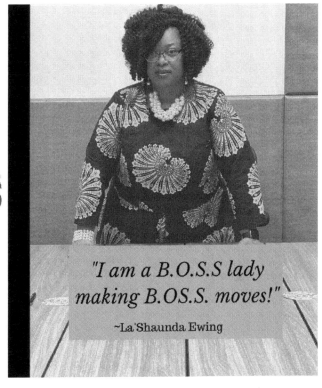

"I am a B.O.S.S lady making B.OS.S. moves!"

~La'Shaunda Ewing

SUCCESS IS A PROCESS

"Not everybody can be famous. But everybody can be great because greatness is determined by service."
~Martin Luther King, Jr.

Success is the accomplishment of an aim or purpose, the good or bad outcome of an undertaking. Yes, even the bad, because failures are some of the best life lessons; you know what to avoid or things you don't want in your future. In my job, sometimes people ask me to do something for them that I may not know how to do. When that happens, I accept, study, and prepare for the task.

"Pride goeth before destruction, and a haughty spirit before a fall.
Proverbs 16:18

Sometimes I must put my pride aside and ask for help. These are times of growth and progress. You will cherish them and pat yourself on the back when the goal is complete. Again, thank yourself for each opportunity GOD presents because He trusts you and the gifts he has placed in you. This is a practice that I want you to consider as a B.O.S.S.

Transferable Skills

Transferable skills are skills you acquire during your education, internships, community service, volunteer activities, or work experience that you bring to future employment settings. Employers are finding transferable skills increasingly valuable in new hires.

Some examples of transferable hard skills include:

- Technical Knowledge (computer skills)
- Education
- Project Management
- Critical Thinking
- Attention to Detail
- Effective Communication (listening)
- Teamwork
- Empathy and Integrity

B.O.S.S. RIGHTS

Exercise - Transferable Skills

When was the last time you reviewed your catalog of skills and talents? Make a list of transferable skills, hobbies, and side hustles you enjoy and skills:

1. _____
   - _____
   - _____
   - _____

2. _____
   - _____
   - _____
   - _____

3. _____
   - _____
   - _____
   - _____

4. _____
   - _____
   - _____
   - _____

5. _____
   - _____
   - _____
   - _____

6. _____
   - _____
   - _____
   - _____

7. _____
   - _____
   - _____
   - _____

Ask yourself: How confident am I in the skills/duties I listed? If I am not feeling confident, how can I get better?

Just because you are a B.O.S.S. does not give you a license to destroy what someone else has built. When you destroy someone else's foundation to create a name for yourself, you ruin their legacy and the platform built for you to stand on. Don't take pride in being that type of leader. With wisdom, respect, and humbleness, you can develop the strength to stand on someone else's shoulders and thank them for being a stepping stone for your success.

It is okay to ask for help if you need it. And if you really want an easy transition, shadow the previous Boss, and pay attention to the areas where you can glean greatness. Also, understand where you can shine brightest by bringing your new ideas for correction and advancement.

SERVICE IS A PRIORITY

So, in everything, do to others what you would have them do to you, for this sums up the Law and the Prophets.
Matthew 7:12

Hey girl, what are you afraid of?

I used to tell myself, "I'm not afraid of nobody. I'm an Aries. We're taught to fight." But on the inside, I would be afraid to look at the truth. I remember driving up to Hoover Dam and beginning to cry. The overwhelming fear was sudden and overtook me. I was not sure why, but with encouragement from my mother, I could continue driving. We had somewhere to go, and I needed that word to keep going.

When I question my actions, I start to procrastinate, and that is a shame.

I've helped others achieve their goals, but when it comes to me, I always find a reason not to act. I had to say to myself and often, "*Girl, you are worthy of everything God has favored you with. You are a B.O.S.S.*" I already had enough to sustain my vision. He has favored me before. It might be impossible for me to do some things, but with God, all things are possible. We got this because HE Got us!

When a person doesn't feel worthy, they procrastinate. At least, that is what happened to me. You can help everybody else's vision, but if you can't walk out your own, what good is that? Where are your B.O.S.S. rights, friend?

Enough of the lies we keep telling ourselves, that our past keeps trying to hold over us, and that I will be like someone else. I am great on my own. I can do whatever I put my mind to, and it is so! That's an exclamation point versus a question mark. We will trust our greatness.

We must take life one day at a time to tear down the strongholds that keep trying to hold us back. Our ancestors dealt with being sold into slavery, molestation, and rape, and Jim crow laws to limit their opportunities. Yet they overcame those horrors and barriers to forge space and grace for us. Is it a roadblock that is keeping you from going higher? I had made my own roadblocks which led to a 10-year stagnation from the time I received the visions. I am just now writing this book and launching my business officially.

Enough of those lies. You're pretty. Nope, you're actually beautiful. You are smart. You don't have to dumb yourself down anymore to make other people feel large. You don't have to let people talk to you crazy so that you can fit in with their crowd. You are a gift to this world, destined to make a difference.

Find the courage to fight the good fight of faith and get out of your comfort zone. Don't wait around for someone to beg you to serve. You can take the first step and watch your talents make room for you.

I treat my service to my Sorority and other commitments like I do the service to my job. I give to my church and community as if I am serving God because it is that important to me. I am a servant-leader who focuses primarily on the growth and well-being of people and the communities to which I belong.

Are you a servant-leader? Be the kind of leader who recognizes and cultivates the talents of those people in your organization. Don't forget to take inventory of the skills of your team and yourself so you know how to guide and advance as a B.O.S.S.

As you prepare for service in any capacity, you must study hard for new opportunities. If you see a situation where an organization is not moving in the best direction or needs a refresher or a change, then B.O.S.S. up! Find out where you can apply your skills, run for office, or volunteer to serve.

Leadership is everyone's job. It can be executed at every level of the organization when the proper processes are in place.

"Be confident, be powerful and make moves like a boss!"

~Jessica Duckett

CONCLUSION

Let us not become weary in doing good, for at the proper time we will reap a harvest if we do not give up.
Galatians 6:9

I went through some things in the process of writing this book. I believe God was trying to make sure I was ready to release this work. Ecclesiastes chapter three says that seasons change. I have changed. As a people pleaser, when God called me into the next season, I had to let some people go.

Let Them Go

You have to be comfortable being a B.O.S.S., knowing that everyone is not fit for your journey. There are people who will tag along with you because of the magnitude of opportunities they see you achieving. Don't let them stop you from moving forward. In your B.O.S.S. season, you don't need people to pat you on your back or approve of what God is doing through you.

God has already approved things in you from birth, and certain people are not appointed to go with you where you are called. It would be insane to stay in the spaces where you felt complacent and comfortable because you cannot take those habits into your next elevation. This is the season of change that you must walk into. If you keep trying to do the same things in the same places expecting different results, you are lying to yourself, and that is the definition of insanity.

Some things in your life have to be torn away because its season has been over for some time. Trust God. Instead of letting the world tell you lies about what success is, understand God's plan. All the necessary resources and blueprints will come with His plan.

But seek ye first the kingdom of God, and all his righteousness, and all these things shall be added unto you.

Matthew 6:33

As a B.O.S.S., you need new opportunities. You cannot keep trying to put newness in old wineskins anymore. God has destroyed those places. Stop trying to put them back together. It will not always be easy. You may cry during some seasons, but Ecclesiastes reminds us there is a time for mourning. Mourn for a moment but keep it moving. You have B.O.S.S. rights you need to achieve.

People are dependent on you at your next level to save their lives. Being built for opportunities, success, and service means you must move out of your way and surrender the familiar. It's not necessary. It has served its purpose. Somebody else will carry it to the next level while you are birthing your next vision.

You are created in God's image. He has called you to higher heights than what you lower yourself to. If you want to be a true B.O.S.S., understand that being busy does not always mean doing good. When you live out what God has called you to, that is when you will help people understand their legacy, and your happiness can be fulfilled.

The Bible says that our ways are not God's ways, and our thoughts are not His thoughts. Are you ready to trust Him completely, no matter what others say or do? I hope so because you are Built for Opportunities, Success, and Service to yourself and this world. (B.O.S.S.). Too often, I have witnessed people forget that they are selected for roles based on the skills and talents they brought to the table.

What does God exceedingly and abundantly want to do in you? When you know your gifts, your place, purpose, and timing, that makes you a B.O.S.S. Remember, to walk in your B.O.S.S. rights, you need to do the following:

1. Create checklists.
2. Get a coach or a mentor to hold you accountable for your success.
3. Have a village of people who understand your plan and that greatness within you must be delivered to the world.

4. Ask your village to pray for and with you and remind you what God says.
5. Speak over yourself based on what God promised you.
6. Stand firm on the shoulders of our ancestors, who paved the way.
7. Celebrate your accomplishment, no matter how small.
8. Let go of the past and the baggage holding you back.
9. Praise Him for how He has kept you and stop believing the lies.
10. Receive the blessings, activate the vision, and walk it out.

You are a B.O.S.S.

Follow these steps, and You are on your way to greatness, purpose, and loving yourself. Just look in the mirror, smile, and tell yourself, "Victory is mine! I am Built for Opportunities, Success, and Service."

ADDITIONAL SCRIPTURE REFERENCES

- Genesis 50:20
- Ephesians 4:26
- James 4:8-10
- Isaiah 38:17
- James 1:12
- Isaiah 41:10
- Romans 8:28
- I John 1:9
- II Corinthians 12:10
- II Corinthians 1:3-4
- Isaiah 43:2
- Mark 2:22
- Galatians 6:9
- Philippians 3:13-14

ABOUT THE AUTHOR

La'Shaunda Ewing is a native of Cincinnati, Ohio. She is an educator, licensed teacher, choir director, entrepreneur, life coach, and event planner.

An IT professional, La'Shaunda has a Bachelor of Science degree from Wilberforce University, a Master of Arts degree from Mount St. Joseph University, a Master's Certification in Project Management from George Washington University, and a host of other certifications.

As a proud life member of Sigma Gamma Rho Sorority, La'Shaunda devotes many hours of service to the Epsilon Lambda Sigma Chapter in Cincinnati.

La'Shaunda is also a licensed minister. She is the owner of Wisdom Flows, LLC., which has a mission to support others in their personal development. The company's motto is "Letting Knowledge and spirit be your guide."

Made in the USA
Middletown, DE
01 September 2024